THE
TITANIC

by
Tom Stacey

**Illustrations by
Maurie Manning and Michael Spackman**

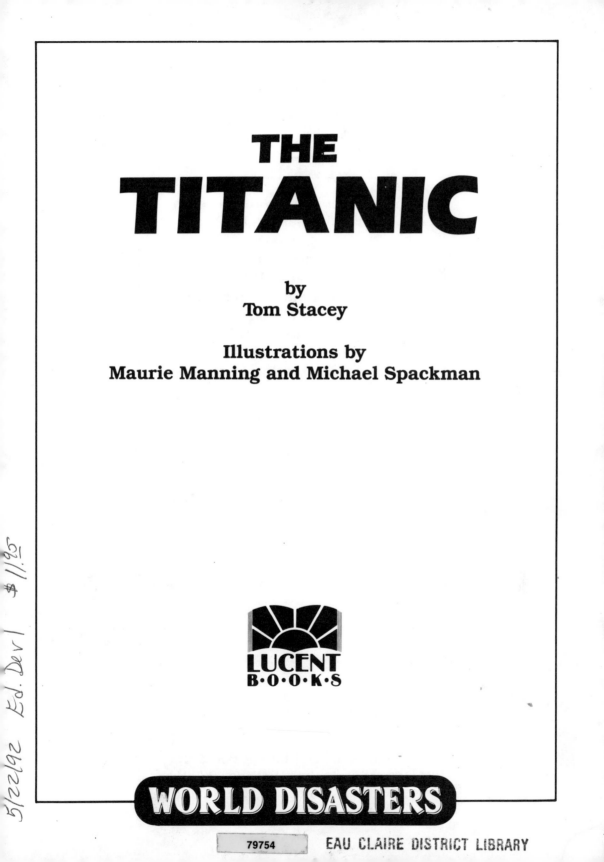

**LUCENT
B·O·O·K·S**

WORLD DISASTERS

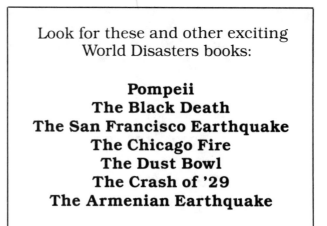

Look for these and other exciting
World Disasters books:

Pompeii
The Black Death
The San Francisco Earthquake
The Chicago Fire
The Dust Bowl
The Crash of '29
The Armenian Earthquake

Library of Congress Cataloging-in-Publication Data

Stacey, Tom, 1960-
     The Titanic / by Thomas Stacey ; illustrations by Maurie Manning and Michael Spackman.
          p.   cm. -- (World disasters)
     Bibliography: p.
     Includes index.
     Summary: An account of the 1914 sinking during her maiden voyage of the luxurious and supposedly unsinkable Titanic, the largest ship in the world at that time.
     ISBN 1-56006-006-9
     1. Titanic (Steamship)--Juvenile literature. 2. Shipwrecks--North Atlantic Ocean--Juvenile literature.   [1. Titanic (Steamship) 2. Ship-wrecks.] I. Manning, Maurie 1960- ill. II. Title III. Series.
G530.T6S79 1989
363.12'3'09163--dc20   89-33553
                                                                      CIP
                                                                      AC

To my Grandparents,
Elmer and Rosemary Stacy,
who were here then,
and Edward and Lucille Harkins,
who are here still.

Table of Contents

Preface
The World Disasters Series

World disasters have always aroused human curiosity. Whenever news of tragedy spreads, we want to learn more about it. We wonder how and why the disaster happened, how people reacted, and whether we might have acted differently. To be sure, disaster evokes a wide range of responses—fear, sorrow, despair, generosity, even hope. Yet from every great disaster, one remarkable truth always seems to emerge: in spite of death, pain, and destruction, the human spirit triumphs.

History is full of great disasters, which arise from a variety of causes. Earthquakes, floods, volcanic eruptions, and other natural events often produce widespread destruction. Just as often, however, people accidentally bring suffering and distress on themselves and other human beings. And many disasters have sinister causes, like human greed, envy, or prejudice.

The disasters included in this series have been chosen not only for their dramatic qualities, but also for their educational value. The reader will learn about the causes and effects of the greatest disasters in history. Technical concepts and interesting anecdotes are explained and illustrated in inset boxes.

But disasters should not be viewed in isolation. To enrich the reader's understanding, these books present historical information about the time period, and interesting facts about the culture in which each disaster occurred. Finally, they teach valuable lessons about human nature. More acts of bravery, cowardice, intelligence, and foolishness are compressed into the few days of a disaster than most people experience in a lifetime.

Dramatic illustrations and evocative narrative lure the reader to distant cities and times gone by. Readers witness the awesome power of an exploding volcano, the magnitude of a violent earthquake, and the hopelessness of passengers on a mighty ship passing to its watery grave. By reliving the events, the reader will see how disaster affects the lives of real people and will gain a deeper understanding of their sorrow, their pain, their courage, and their hope.

Introduction
The Maiden Voyage

On April 10, 1912, the Royal Mail Ship *Titanic* began her maiden voyage, steaming out of Southampton, England, on her way across the North Atlantic to New York. Three years in the making, the *Titanic* was the largest and most luxurious ship in the world. Her first voyage was the major social event of the year. Many of the world's wealthiest and most famous figures signed on for the trip.

This gigantic ship provided the best that technology had to offer. First-class passengers enjoyed the finest rooms, food, and service ever seen afloat. The heated swimming pool, gymnasium, squash court, and grand ballroom were just a few of the ship's uncommon pleasures. Expertly crafted and richly decorated, the *Titanic* was the finest example of turn-of-the-century elegance. Her captain and crew were the most capable sailors in England.

Her design was praised as a marvel of engineering. One magazine labeled her "practically unsinkable," and soon the *Titanic* became known as the "unsinkable ship." By the time they embarked on her maiden voyage, many of the 2,227 passengers and crew on board actually believed the *Titanic* could not be sunk. They were so certain that when the *Titanic* struck an iceberg at 11:40 P.M. on April 14, four days after leaving Southampton, many on board were unconcerned. Even when the crew began telling passengers to put on life jackets, many remained unconvinced. As the first lifeboats were being lowered, almost empty, to the icy waters below, most passengers scoffed at the idea that the *Titanic* could possibly sink.

Yet by 2:20 A.M., April 15, the "impossible" had happened. The unsinkable *Titanic* had sunk. Few passengers made it into the ship's twenty lifeboats, and the loss of life shocked the world: 1,522 people drowned. Only 705 were rescued. It was the greatest peacetime disaster in maritime history.

The sinking of the *Titanic* has become the most famous shipwreck in history. That is partly because so many lives were lost. But it is also because the *Titanic* was more than just a ship. It was a symbol of the future.

The early part of the twentieth century, when the *Titanic* was built, was an exciting time. It was a time when steam engines, steel mills, railroads, steamships, cars, radios, and the first airplanes seemed to be making the world a smaller, more comfortable, and better place to live.

The *Titanic* was thought to be the greatest technological achievement of its day. She was enormous and luxurious. She had taken three years to build, and her ingenious design made her "unsinkable." Yet only four days into her first voyage, this masterpiece lay at the bottom of the ocean. When the *Titanic* went down, many hopes and dreams went down with her.

Titanic's **Place in History**

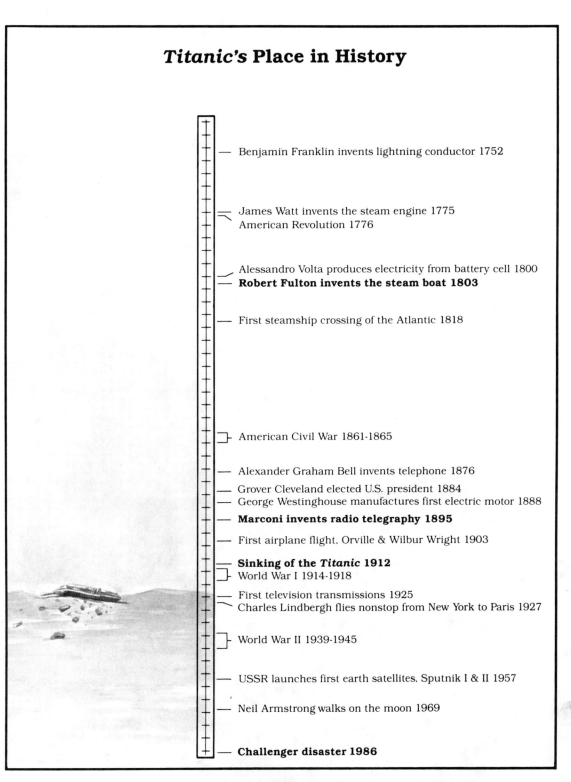

Benjamin Franklin invents lightning conductor 1752

James Watt invents the steam engine 1775
American Revolution 1776

Alessandro Volta produces electricity from battery cell 1800
Robert Fulton invents the steam boat 1803

First steamship crossing of the Atlantic 1818

American Civil War 1861-1865

Alexander Graham Bell invents telephone 1876
Grover Cleveland elected U.S. president 1884
George Westinghouse manufactures first electric motor 1888
Marconi invents radio telegraphy 1895

First airplane flight, Orville & Wilbur Wright 1903

Sinking of the *Titanic* 1912
World War I 1914-1918

First television transmissions 1925
Charles Lindbergh flies nonstop from New York to Paris 1927

World War II 1939-1945

USSR launches first earth satellites, Sputnik I & II 1957

Neil Armstrong walks on the moon 1969

Challenger disaster 1986

One
The Home Port

Without warning, the huge ship let out a long, loud blast of steam, signaling the final call for boarding passengers. The sound echoed across the harbor before it gave way to seagull cries and the clanking of buoys. It was April 10, 1912, and the dock in Southampton, England, was crowded with ticketed passengers. They were eager to board the R.M.S. *Titanic* for her maiden voyage to New York. Their families and friends filled the wharf. They hugged, kissed, shook hands, and said their final goodbyes before the passengers boarded the gigantic ship.

On the ship's **bridge**, the bearded, stately-looking captain was conferring with two other gentlemen. One was Thomas Andrews, the chief designer of the *Titanic*. The other was J. Bruce Ismay, president and general manager of the White Star Line, the shipping company that owned the big new ship. It was Ismay who had first proposed building the *Titanic*, the biggest and most luxurious ship ever. Both he and Andrews would be traveling first class on the maiden voyage.

The White Star Line had awarded command of the *Titanic* to Captain Smith, age sixty-two, in recognition of his long service to the company. In more than forty years on the high seas, Smith had a nearly perfect safety record. Now he was observing the boarding operation to make sure that everything went smoothly before he commanded his crew to shove off.

An elderly couple walked slowly up the lower **gangway** that led to the first-class compartments. They were Mr. and Mrs. Isidor Straus, owners of Macy's Department Store in New York City. Mr. Straus had also served in the U.S. Congress. Now the elderly couple were enjoying their retirement by taking in such world-class events as the *Titanic's* first voyage. A servant and maid accompanied them.

At the foot of this gangway, cameras clicked, flash bulbs popped, and newspaper reporters jostled for position. There a gentlemen in a pin-striped overcoat and black felt bowler hat escorted a young, pregnant woman, who was wearing an elegant fur coat. This well-dressed gentleman was John Jacob Astor IV. At the age of fifty-six, Astor was one of the wealthiest men in the world.

The woman at Astor's side was his young wife, Madeleine. Ever since he had married her a year earlier, when she was only eighteen, the newspaper reporters had hounded them mercilessly. In fact, the Astors were just returning from a long trip to Egypt, where they had gone to escape the press.

Next to the dock, where hundreds of people still milled about, the *Titanic* looked like something that had sailed in from a land of giants. It was the largest ship that had ever been built.

To this day, the *Titanic* ranks as one of the most luxurious ships ever built. As journalist Sir Philip Gibbs put it:

> *All that the genius of modern life has invented for comfort and adornment was lavished upon her…all that wealth and art can attain in splendour was given to her decoration…. The richest man on earth would not lack a single comfort that his wealth might buy.*

Many of the most prominent people in the world had signed on for her maiden voyage. It was the most glamorous social event of the year. Among the first-class passengers was Benjamin Guggenheim from Philadelphia, whose family had made millions in the mining business. Also from Philadelphia was the Widener family, who had made its fortune manufacturing streetcars. Mr. John B. Thayer, an executive with the Pennsylvania Railroad, was traveling with Mrs. Thayer and their seventeen-year-old son, Jack. Henry Harper of Harper's Publishing Company was on board, as was Harry Molson, the Canadian beer-brewing giant.

Other distinguished first-class passengers included Major Archibald Butt, a military aide to President William H. Taft; William Thomas Stead, a well-known British editor and free thinker; and Denver millionairess Margaret "Molly" Brown.

On the dock, servants of these first-class passengers pushed carts loaded with suitcases and heavy trunks toward an electric crane, which lifted the luggage onto the ship. Alongside these servants, second- and third-class passengers dragged their own luggage to the loading crane. Many, like Frederick and Augusta Goodwin and their six children, had two or three large trunks, which contained all of their personal belongings.

Frederick Goodwin was an electrical engineer from London. He was moving his family to Niagara Falls, New York. His brother Thomas already lived there and had written to Frederick about a job opening at a large power plant. To the Goodwin family, the maiden voyage of the *Titanic* was not a social event. It was a way to get to a new life in a new land.

It was just a lucky coincidence that they happened to be on the *Titanic*. The Goodwins were originally booked on another liner. They were transferred

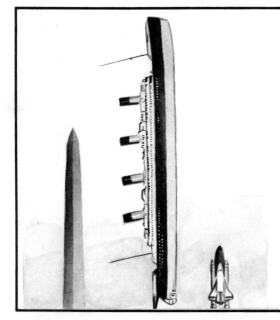

HOW BIG WAS IT?

In 1912, the *Titanic* was the biggest ship ever built. She was 882 feet long (264.6 meters). If set on one end, the *Titanic* would be 300 feet (90 meters) taller than the Washington Monument. It would be almost five times as tall as a space shuttle on its booster rocket.

This gigantic ship weighed 46,000 tons. A single link of the ship's anchor chain weighed 175 pounds (79 kilograms), and 20 strong horses were needed just to haul each of her three anchors to the shipyard.

The *Titanic's* three coal-powered steam engines were each as big as a three-story house. Her four smokestacks (one was for decoration only) rose 62 feet (19 meters) above the ship's deck, and each one was wide enough for two train engines to drive through.

to the *Titanic* when the other ship's voyage was canceled due to a coal miners' strike.

Like the Goodwins, most third-class passengers were **immigrating** to America. Many of them had used their life's savings and sold their homes and other possessions to pay for their passage. Of the 1,320 passengers on the *Titanic*, 712 of them were traveling third class. Although that was more than half of all the passengers, third-class quarters took up less than one tenth of the amount of space reserved for first and second class.

The rest of the ship offered a combination of comforts never before seen on board a ship. The *Titanic* had electric elevators, barber shops with automatic shampoo and hair-drying machines, and darkrooms for photographers. First- and second-class travelers could dine in their choice of several fine restaurants. They could even swim in the first heated pool ever built on a ship.

The finest rooms on board were the two suites on B Deck known as the Millionaire Suites. Each suite was 50 feet long (15 meters), with a large parlor, two luxurious bedrooms, a full bathroom, and a private promenade deck.

Other first-class suites were not as large, but almost as elegant. Passengers staying in them could have easily forgotten they were on a ship. The suites were lavishly decorated in the style of the best hotels in Europe. On other ships, pipes and wires were visible inside first-class cabins. On the *Titanic*, these were covered by richly paneled or plastered walls. First-class passengers gazed through a bedroom window rather than through the usual **porthole** when they looked outside.

The second-class cabins were located near the rear of the ship on Decks C, D, and E. By second-class standards, they were extremely comfortable. Each suite had two marble-topped sinks, an electric heater, and a porthole.

The owners of the *Titanic* had spared no expense on their first- and second-class patrons. But the White Star Line's real profits were expected to come from the great number of immigrants and other third-class travelers.

The rooms for all 712 third-class passengers were located below the *fore* and *aft* decks, far in the *bow* and *stern* of the ship. Third-class travelers were not allowed in many parts of the ship. At most times, locked gates prevented them from entering areas reserved for first and second class.

Such gates were standard equipment on most passenger ships at this time. They dated back to earlier days when many ships carried both passengers and livestock. Then, the gates were used to confine cattle and other animals to the rear of the ship. That is why the rear section of a ship is still referred to as *steerage*.

Third-class passengers probably did not complain, however. Their rooms were comfortable, and they were furnished as nicely as second-class rooms on most ships. The eight-member Goodwin family probably took two cabins with four beds each. These cabins, located at the stern of the ship, were reserved for third-class families.

THE GRAND TOUR

Before the *Titanic* departed, all passengers and guests were permitted to take a grand tour. Near the middle of the top deck, or Boat Deck, was the gymnasium. Reserved for first-class passengers only, it was equipped with rowing machines, stationary bicycles, and all the newest fitness equipment.

Other facilities, such as the swimming pool, saunas, massage rooms, and a regulation-size squash court, were open to both first- and second-class guests.

Not far from the gymnasium was the grand staircase. This was something every passenger wanted to see. The stairway was located in the forward part of the ship, and connected the top

Grand Staircase

First-class Lounge

First-class Stateroom

six decks. It was covered by an ornate dome of glass and wrought-iron. The top flight of stairs featured carved-oak handrails and elaborate, wrought-iron rail supports. Halfway down this flight, a huge clock flanked by bronze figures was built into the wall.

The steps widened gradually as they descended to the B Deck. There, near the staircase, was the first-class lounge. Its ceiling and walls were covered with elaborate plaster details patterned after the Palace of Versailles in France. It had a cloak room, a bar, a reading room, and several alcoves where people could gather to have tea, write letters, or chat with friends.

Two
The Birth of a Giant

The *Titanic* was like a small town at sea. In fact, the different classes of people on board were much like the different classes in a typical European city or town. For example, most of the space on the ship was reserved for a relatively small number of first-class passengers. They represented the wealthiest and most successful members of society.

Among the people in second class were many teachers, doctors, and other professionals who made up the growing middle class. Like the first-class passengers, most people in second class were looking forward to the voyage on the *Titanic* as an exciting vacation.

The majority of passengers on board the *Titanic*, like the majority of people in Europe, belonged to the working class. They were not on vacation. Rather, most of them were immigrating to America. In 1912, American industry and westward expansion offered more opportunities than their European homelands offered. The dense population and rigid class structure made it difficult to get ahead in Europe.

For nearly a century, they had provided cheap labor to manufacture products, mine coal, stoke steam engines, and load ships. They had made the **Industrial Revolution** possible, but they did not have much to show for it. Most of them lived in run-down houses on dark, narrow streets in the slums of industrial cities.

Gradually, however, the Industrial Revolution created greater opportunities for the working classes. Recent inventions such as typewriters, **wireless** telegraphs, sewing machines, telephones, and electric lights made people's work easier and saved them time.

People and goods were beginning to move more rapidly as well. In 1903, Henry Ford built his first car in Detroit. Late that same year, Wilbur and Orville Wright flew in the first airplane at Kitty Hawk, North Carolina. And the steam engine, which had opened up vast areas of land to the railroads in the nineteenth century, was finally proving practical in large ships, too.

Transatlantic steamships could carry goods and people between the United States and Europe faster than ever. Crossing the Atlantic by sailing ship had been a trying and often dangerous six-week voyage. On the new steamships, it was a comfortable six- or seven-day cruise.

Steamships also made transatlantic travel affordable. Members of the working class welcomed the opportunity to immigrate to the United States. They had heard about free homesteads and bountiful resources in the "new world." They had heard the story of John Jacob Astor, the great grandfather of John Jacob Astor IV, who had immigrated to America and built a family fortune trading furs. Confident that they too could build better lives for themselves, millions of Europeans went to the United States in the early 1900s with high hopes and dreams of success.

BUILDING THE *TITANIC*

The *Titanic* was built at the shipyards of Harland and Wolff in Belfast, Ireland. As it was being built, it sat on giant runners on a concrete ramp that angled toward the water.

Building the ship was a brutal job. Workers climbed hundreds of feet of scaffolding erected around the huge skeleton of the ship. The riveting crews riveted great steel plates together to form the ship's hull. Getting paid by the number of rivets they put in encouraged them to work fast. They typically started work at 6:00 in the morning and worked until 5:30 at night. A team of four men could put in about two hundred rivets a day.

After more than three million rivets were in place, the *Titanic* was ready to launch. First, the runners on which it sat were well greased. Then the giant ship was given a shove by a hydraulic *ram*. The *Titanic* slid back on its runners until it hit the water. At that moment, a chorus of cheers erupted from the thousands of workers and spectators who had gathered to witness this historic moment.

The increased traffic between Europe and the United States created fierce competition among steamship companies for this growing market. That is what brought J. Bruce Ismay, chairman of the White Star Line, and William Pirrie, chairman of Harland & Wolff, an Irish shipbuilding firm, together. The two businessmen met one night for dinner to discuss ways to make the White Star Line more competitive. They came up with a plan, drew some sketches, and the idea for the *Titanic* was born.

Actually, their plan was to build three huge ocean liners. The enormous size of these ships would make them a little slower than some steamships. But the luxuries they would offer would more than compensate for their slower speed.

To launch their dream, Ismay and Pirrie needed someone to help finance the plan. They convinced American industrialist J. Pierpont Morgan to support them.

The project got under way in the spring of 1909. More than three thousand men at the Belfast shipyards of Harland & Wolff began work on the first two of the White Star ships, the *Olympic* and her slightly larger sister ship, the *Titanic*.

When she was finished, the *Titanic* had room for 2,500 passengers. In order to make room for this many passengers and still provide all the luxuries for its first-class guests, the owners of the *Titanic* had decided to equip the ship with only sixteen wooden lifeboats and four canvas collapsible boats—enough to carry about half of the people on board.

It seemed a wise choice at the time. It was more than the minimum required by British law for a ship the size of the *Titanic*. Besides, she was designed to be extremely safe. The **hull** of the *Titanic* was constructed of two solid layers of steel, each an inch thick. In addition, its unique design divided the ship into sixteen watertight compartments. If three or four of these compartments filled with water, the *Titanic* could stay afloat. So impressive was this design that the ship soon became known as the "unsinkable" *Titanic*. Surely lifeboats would never be needed on this ship. They just took up valuable space on the Boat Deck.

THE *TITANIC'S* UNSINKABLE DESIGN

Fifteen watertight **bulkheads**, or support walls, divided the *Titanic* into sixteen separate sections. Each bulkhead extended from the bottom of the ship up to the fifth deck, well above the water line. Even if four of these sections filled with water, the ship could still float.

The doors in these bulkheads were also watertight, and they could be raised or lowered by an electric switch on the bridge. In addition, powerful pumps in each of the sections could quickly pump out any water that the *Titanic* took on.

HOW A STEAMSHIP WORKS

A steamship uses the power of a steam engine to turn propellers, which drive the ship through the water. The steam engine works by converting heat into mechanical energy. This takes place in a *boiler* (1), where water is boiled into steam. As the water turns to steam, it expands. The expanding steam creates pressure in a *cylinder* (2). The pressure in the cylinder pushes a *piston* (3) back and forth. The piston is attached to a *crankshaft* (4). As the piston moves back and forth, it turns the crankshaft. The crankshaft is attached to the *propeller* (5). And as the propeller turns, it pushes the ship through the water.

After three years of work, on May 31, 1911, the *Titanic* was ready to launch. The consensus among the press was that the new ship was a triumph of technology.

Preparations for a maiden voyage included testing the new ship's capabilities and limits. These testing procedures, or **trials**, normally took several weeks to complete. During that time, the captain and crew gradually learned how to operate and maneuver the new ship at full speed.

In the case of the *Titanic*, however, the trials were conducted in just one afternoon off the coast of Belfast. According to records, the ship simply steamed a short distance beyond the harbor at eighteen **knots**, did one big U-turn, and went back to the Harland & Wolff shipyards. It was as if the *Titanic*'s grand size and luxury put her outside the normal rules.

The crew was so confident of the ship's safety that it even skipped the normal lifeboat drills. Though lowering lifeboats in an emergency could be awkward for an untrained crew, no one anticipated an emergency on board the *Titanic*.

THE *TITANIC*

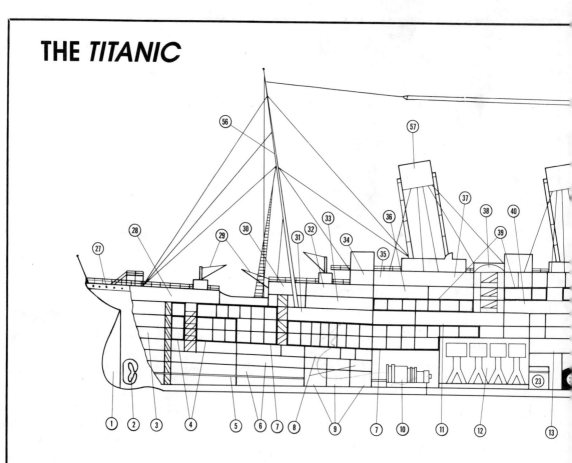

Rudder - 1
Propeller - 2
Cargo Holds - 3
Third Class Berths/Steerage - 4
Propeller Shaft Tunnel - 5
Refrigerated Cargo - 6
State Rooms, 2nd Class - 7
Ship's Provisions - 8
Fresh Water Tanks - 9
Steam Turbine Engine - 10
Kitchen, 1st & 2nd Class - 11
Reciprocating (Piston) Steam Engines - 12
Kitchen, 3rd Class - 13
Dining Saloon, 1st Class - 14
Dining Saloon, 3rd Class - 15
First Class Reception - 16
Turkish Bath - 17
Mail Room - 18
Bulkhead - 19
Fire Fighters' Passage - 20

Motor Cars - 21
Hull - 22
Boilers - 23
Coal - 24
Swimming Pool - 25
Squash Court - 26
Porthole - 27
Smoking Room, 3rd Class - 28
Cranes - 29
Second Class Entrance - 30
Dining Saloon, 2nd Class - 31
Smoking Room, 2nd Class - 32
Library - 33
Veranda Cafe - 34
Bar - 35
Restaurant - 36
Smoking Room, 1st Class - 37
First Class Vestibule and Staircase - 38
State Rooms, 1st Class - 39
Maids' & Valets' Dining Saloon - 40

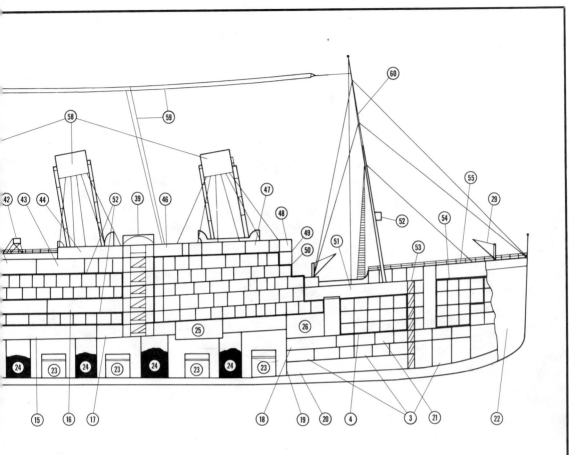

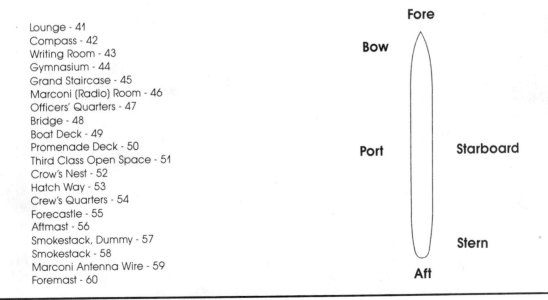

Lounge - 41
Compass - 42
Writing Room - 43
Gymnasium - 44
Grand Staircase - 45
Marconi (Radio) Room - 46
Officers' Quarters - 47
Bridge - 48
Boat Deck - 49
Promenade Deck - 50
Third Class Open Space - 51
Crow's Nest - 52
Hatch Way - 53
Crew's Quarters - 54
Forecastle - 55
Aftmast - 56
Smokestack, Dummy - 57
Smokestack - 58
Marconi Antenna Wire - 59
Foremast - 60

Fore

Bow

Port   Starboard

Stern

Aft

Three
A Date with Destiny

Most passengers boarding the ship at Southampton on April 10, 1912, had no doubts about the crew's ability to maneuver the *Titanic*. A mood of celebration grew as the crowd on the wharf shouted and waved, and powerful tugboats nudged the gigantic ship out into the channel. There her boilers growled, and the ship's engines roared to life. Passengers lined the deck of the *Titanic* and waved back to their friends on the dock.

Just minutes into her maiden voyage, the *Titanic* passed the *New York*, a much smaller ship that was still tied to the dock. As the *Titanic* steamed by, the huge ropes holding the *New York* to the dock snapped one by one. The *New York* was pulled without warning away from the dock and towards the *Titanic*.

Captain Smith quickly cut his main engines. But still the *New York* drew toward the larger ship, and a collision seemed inevitable. At the last second, Captain Smith gave a small thrust to the engines. This created a current away from the *Titanic* and pushed the *New York* away from the huge ship. Finally a tugboat intervened and pushed the *New York* back toward the dock. Too close for comfort, the *Titanic* and the *New York* had missed each other by a few feet.

Oddly enough, a similar incident had occurred on the *Olympic's* maiden voyage. The *Titanic's* sister ship had actually collided with a smaller ship and sustained damage to her hull. The captain on the *Olympic* at the time was none other than E.J. Smith, the man now at the **helm** of the *Titanic*. Both incidents suggested that there was still much to be learned about maneuvering these gigantic, new ships.

It didn't take long for most passengers to forget the disturbing scene in the Southampton harbor. They were busy enjoying the luxuries the big ship had to offer.

Some sunned themselves on the deck, others wrote letters, read books, or just sat and watched the sea. No matter what class they were traveling, all the passengers seemed to be enjoying themselves.

The first-class passengers were given special treatment. The 290 stewards and stewardesses were dedicated to meeting their every need. Chefs prepared special dishes to be served in the

Titanic's first-class dining room, where Italian and French waiters attended to the guests.

While sampling the exquisite food, these elite passengers also enjoyed the companionship of other well-to-do travelers. Some renewed acquaintances from earlier cruises. While they dined, they were entertained by a twelve-piece orchestra.

After dinner, many of the men went to the first-class smoking room. Its rich mahogany paneling, open fireplace, and large stained-glass windows may have reminded them of their men's clubs back home. Many played bridge, or, if the stewards didn't object, poker. Among the first-class passengers were a few professional gamblers, looking for easy winnings among the rich vacationers.

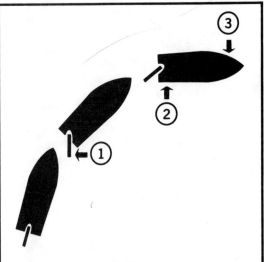

STEERING A SHIP

Steering a ship is not like steering a car. Travelling at full speed, it would take a ship the size of the *Titanic* more than a mile to complete a ninety-degree turn.

A ship is steered by a ***sternwheel*** located on the ship's bridge. The sternwheel is connected by a series of shafts to the **rudder** at the rear of the ship. To turn the ship to the *right*, the rudder must be turned to the *right* (1). As the ship moves forward, the water hitting the rudder pushes the stern of the ship to the *left* (2). As the stern moves to the left, the bow points *right*, and the ship turns in that direction (3).

The second- and third-class passengers also enjoyed dining on the *Titanic*. Although it was not nearly as fancy as in first class, there was plenty of good food, and the service was far better than anything they were accustomed to.

On Sunday, April 14, after four days at sea, the *Titanic* was steaming through the arctic waters of the North Atlantic. The weather was normal for April—cool but clear. There were no storms on the horizon. The big ship was making good time, and Captain Smith was running her full steam ahead.

The only hint that conditions were not ideal came in a wireless message received by Captain Smith. It was a warning from a ship called the *Baltic* that ice had been sighted in the area. He

received the message about 1:30 P.M. and shortly after that showed it to J. Bruce Ismay, the president of White Star Lines. Ismay was dining in the first-class dining room at the time Captain Smith handed him the message. Ismay read it and then stuffed it in his pocket. Neither he nor the Captain seemed worried.

Perhaps they would have been more concerned if they had seen the ice warning that the *Titanic*'s wireless operators received a few minutes later. In fact, that was the third such warning. As the day progressed, the wireless operators received three more.

Normally, navigation messages were passed from the wireless operators to the crew and eventually to the captain. But the *Titanic* had no set procedure for relaying the messages. On this day, only a few of the ice warnings actually reached the captain. In fact, no single person saw all six ice warnings.

If all six warnings had been plotted on a chart, they would have shown an unmistakable, oblong wall of ice running north and south directly in the path of the *Titanic*. But no one mapped out the warnings. The only precaution taken by Captain Smith was an order to the lookouts to be aware of icebergs, especially **growlers** — icebergs that are almost totally underwater.

At 9:40 P.M., a ship named the *Rappahannock* delivered the sixth warning. It had just steamed cautiously through an ice field and sustained damage to its **rudder**. The *Rappahannock* sent this message to the *Titanic*: "Have just passed through heavy ice field and several icebergs." The *Titanic* replied: "Message received. Thanks. Good night."

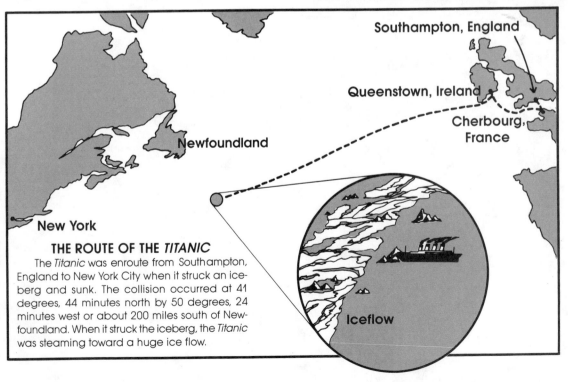

THE ROUTE OF THE *TITANIC*

The *Titanic* was enroute from Southampton, England to New York City when it struck an iceberg and sunk. The collision occurred at 41 degrees, 44 minutes north by 50 degrees, 24 minutes west or about 200 miles south of Newfoundland. When it struck the iceberg, the *Titanic* was steaming toward a huge ice flow.

Southampton, England

Queenstown, Ireland

Cherbourg, France

Newfoundland

New York

Iceflow

On Sunday night there was no moon and no wind, and the sky was full of sparkling stars. The sea was unusually calm and flat. As the temperature dropped to 30 degrees Fahrenheit (-1.1 degrees Celsius), a slight fog formed over the water.

In the **crow's nest** of the *Titanic*, lookouts Fred Fleet and Reginald Lee were keeping watch. So far it had been a routine evening. They were on the last half hour of their two-hour watch, and they were looking forward to the midnight shift change, when they could retire to their warm bunks below.

During their watch, they had commented once or twice about the bitter cold. Otherwise, they just gazed out into the night, searching the dark, glassy waters. As strange as it may seem, the well-equipped *Titanic* had no binoculars in her crow's nest. So the lookouts were forced to scan the horizon with unaided eyes. And what they saw was normal for a moonless night—nothing but sea and stars.

Then at about 11:40 P.M., Fleet suddenly spied something. At first he thought it was about the size of two dining tables put together. Soon he knew it was larger. Fleet automatically rang the ship's warning bell three times, then telephoned the bridge.

"Iceberg right ahead," he said.

On the bridge, Sixth Officer James Moody relayed the news to First Officer Murdoch, who had taken charge when Captain Smith retired for the evening. Murdoch was an experienced seaman, and he acted swiftly. He immediately phoned the engine room and ordered the engines stopped and then put in reverse. He then told **Quartermaster** Robert Hitchens to turn the wheel "hard-a-**starboard**," which would turn the ship to **port**, or left. As he was giving

these orders, he flipped the switch to shut the watertight doors in the hull. Then he waited.

The huge ship did not react as quickly as the men who piloted her. For about thirty seconds, the *Titanic* continued steaming straight ahead. Finally the ship began turning slightly to the left. It seemed to Fleet that she had turned just in time. From the crow's nest, it appeared the *Titanic* had safely swung wide of the berg, and the huge chunk of ice was gliding harmlessly by the starboard, or right side.

Fleet would have thought differently had he been in boiler room No. 6, near the front of the ship. There fireman Fred Barrett and Assistant Second Engineer James Hesketh were talking near the entrance to the boiler room. Suddenly an alarm went off and the red warning light above the doorway began flashing. Seconds later, the wall on the right side of the room gave way with a crash, and a rush of seawater began cascading in around the pipes and machinery. The two men jumped out of the boiler room just before the huge, watertight door slammed shut behind them, sealing the room off from the rest of the ship.

Meanwhile, on the bridge, Murdoch felt a jarring motion, as if the ship had come into port too fast and bumped against a dock. Then he heard a grinding noise from far below. Captain Smith heard it too, and he was out of his room and onto the bridge in an instant.

"Mr. Murdoch, what was that?" he asked.

"An iceberg sir," Murdoch replied. "I was going hard-a-port around it, but she was too close. I could not do anymore. I have closed the watertight doors."

WHAT IS AN ICEBERG?

An iceberg is a huge chunk of ice that has broken away from a glacier and floats in the sea. It consists mainly of crystalized snow that gets harder with age. Most icebergs are over a thousand years old.

Icebergs come in all shapes and sizes, but many tower more than 200 feet (60 meters) above the water and weigh as much as six million tons. Only about one ninth of an iceberg's entire mass shows above the surface.

The iceberg believed to have sunk the *Titanic* rose about 100 feet (30 meters) above the water. A massive 800 feet (240 meters) of solid ice lurked invisibly beneath the surface.

The front of the ship had shot clear of the iceberg as the *Titanic* swung to the left. As it turned, however, its right front side scraped a submerged portion of the enormous berg—which probably weighed about twenty times more than the ship.

The *Titanic* would have steamed headlong into the iceberg at 22 knots, about 23 miles per hour (37 kilometers per hour), were it not for Murdoch's quick orders. But with such a short warning from the crow's nest, it was impossible to avoid contact entirely. As it was, the collision seemed like nothing more than a glancing blow, and it was over in about ten seconds.

Most passengers were already in bed, the warmest place to be on such a cold night, and did not notice a thing. Among the few travelers and crew members who were still awake, hardly anyone thought anything was wrong.

In the first-class smoking room, some men were playing cards. They detected a slight jolt, but they ignored it and went on with their card game. Others also remembered the sensation. It seemed to Mrs. J. Stuart White that the *Titanic* was "rolling over about a thousand marbles." Lady Duff Gordon said it was "as though somebody had drawn a giant finger along the side of the ship." Another passenger didn't feel anything, but heard a sound "like a piece of cloth being torn."

Closer to the front of the ship, one of the firemen was awakened by the collision. Climbing out of bed, he went out to look on the deck and saw that it was covered with small pieces of broken ice.

"Oh, we have struck an iceberg," he said to himself. "That's nothing." Then he returned to his bunk and went back to sleep.

In one of the boiler rooms, a hungry workman was disappointed when his bowl of soup fell from a piece of machinery where it had been warming up. In another part of the ship, a man was startled by a chunk of ice that fell through the open porthole into his cabin.

But Thomas Andrews, designer of the *Titanic*, did not notice the collision at all. He was in his cabin going over the blueprints of his greatest achievement,

looking for slight imperfections that needed fixing. One flaw he noticed was that there were too many screws in the hat hooks in the first-class staterooms. He made a note to have one screw removed from each.

Andrews was not yet aware of a greater flaw in his finest creation. This one was a long gash in the starboard side of her steel hull. It was not something he could fix.

Much more noticeable than the collision was the silence that followed. Captain Smith had immediately ordered the engines shut down, halting the ship's motion through the water. The steady hum the passengers had become accustomed to over the previous four days was silenced, and their curiosity was awakened.

Throughout the ship, they began investigating. In first class, passengers were crawling out of their warm beds, putting bathrobes on over their pajamas, and wandering out into the hallway to ask the stewards what the problem was. The stewards didn't know. "There is no cause for alarm," said one.

Some third-class passengers in the front of the ship didn't need to ask the stewards. One man, troubled by the sudden pause, hopped out of his bunk and found about an inch of water on the floor. By the time he was fully dressed, the water was ankle high and rising evenly.

Soon the ship was alive with activity, and rumors began to circulate.

"Don't be afraid," one member of the crew said to a passenger. "We've only been cutting a whale in two."

Someone else said they had broken a propeller and would have to return to Belfast for repairs. Another story was that they had run aground just off the Banks of Newfoundland. Others heard that the ship had struck a "little" iceberg, but there was no damage, and they would soon be on their way. Another story was that Captain Smith was slowing the ship down because an iceberg had been sighted, and he didn't want to hit it.

But soon people realized that the ship had at least come close to an iceberg. A huge chunk of ice had fallen onto the starboard deck and was attracting a crowd. Still, the ice caused no alarm, but was regarded as a curiosity. People danced around it and joked about putting pieces of it in their drinks. One of the ship's workers broke off a chunk and slipped it under the covers of a mate who was still in bed.

Captain Smith was not taking it so lightly. After the collision, he and First Officer Murdoch had run from the **wheelhouse** out onto the deck to look for the iceberg, but it had already disappeared into the night. Returning to the bridge, the captain sent one of his officers to look for damage. Then he checked the **commutator**, a small instrument mounted with the ship's compass, that indicated how level the ship was.

"Oh my God!" said Smith.

The commutator showed that the ship was already leaning five degrees starboard. Smith had just sent an order to the *Titanic's* carpenter that he **sound** the ship to determine how much water they were taking on.

At that moment, the carpenter burst into the wheelhouse. He had already checked the condition of the ship, and he was alarmed by what his instruments told him — the *Titanic* was filling up fast.

The captain then sent for Thomas Andrews. When Andrews arrived on the bridge, the two men made a quick tour of the bow of the ship to see the damage for themselves. They soon learned the worst.

Four
Women and Children First

Andrews knew every nook and cranny of the *Titanic*. As he and Captain Smith toured the ship, they made mental notes of what they saw. On E Deck, they found that the squash court was filling up rapidly; water was now up to the foul line. Crew members reported that the mail room on F Deck was completely flooded, and bags of mail were floating up to the next deck. Seawater was squirting into boiler room No. 5 from a jagged hole a few inches in diameter. It was coming in much faster, they knew, in boiler room No. 6, where Barrett and Hesketh had jumped out just as the door slammed shut behind them.

Adding it all up, Captain Smith and Andrews figured there had to be a 300-foot (90 meter) tear along the starboard hull. This meant the sea was pouring into the six forward compartments. The ship's powerful pumps had been turned on, but water was coming in much faster than they could pump it back out.

Although the bulkheads were sealed "watertight" to well above the water line, they were open at the top. Like in a tipped ice cube tray, as each compartment filled with water, it overflowed into the next compartment.

It was serious. Both men knew the "unsinkable" ship was doomed to sink. It was only a matter of time. By midnight, about twenty minutes after the collision, Captain Smith gave the order to get the lifeboats ready. He had to accept the horrible fact that this ship, of all ships, was going down beneath him. He knew it was his duty now to save as many lives as possible, so he gave the call to man the lifeboats. On ordinary

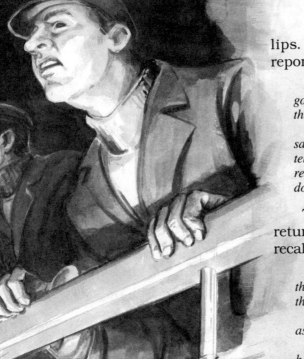

lips. Bride later told his story to a reporter from the *New York Times*:

> *I was standing by Phillips telling him to go to bed when the Captain put his head in the cabin.*
> *"We've struck an iceberg," the Captain said. "And I'm having an inspection made to tell us what it has done for us. You better get ready to put out a call for assistance. But don't send it until I tell you."*

Ten minutes later, the captain returned to the wireless cabin. As Bride recalled, Smith showed no sign of alarm:

> *"Send the call for assistance," ordered the Captain, barely putting his head in the door.*
> *"What call should I send?" Phillips asked.*
> *"The regulation international call for help. Just that."*
> *Then the Captain was gone. Phillips began to send CQD. He flashed away at it and joked as he did so. All of us made light of the disaster.*

Phillips was sending the traditional signal for distress, *CQD*, when the captain came back once again. Bride recalled:

> *"What are you sending?" he asked.*
> *"CQD," Phillips replied.*
> *The humor of the situation appealed to me. I cut in with a little remark that made us all laugh, including the Captain.*
> *"Send SOS," I said. "It's the new call, and it may be your last chance to send it."*

So the world's first *SOS* signal was sent from the *Titanic* at about 12:45 A.M., April 15, 1912. As they joked and laughed in the wireless cabin, Phillips sent the unbelievable call out to the world:

> *Have struck an iceberg. We are badly damaged.* Titanic. *Position 41 degrees, 44'N., 50 degrees 24' W.*

ships, this was a routine order the captain could make with confidence. But the *Titanic* was no ordinary ship.

Now the crew's lack of preparation began to show. No one knew exactly where to go or what to do when the call to the lifeboats was made. Adding to the confusion, it was impossible to hear a word anyone said on the Boat Deck because of the sound of steam escaping through the smokestacks. With the engines shut down, the boilers would explode unless the engineers let all the steam out. Releasing the pent-up steam was causing a deafening roar.

As his officers tried to establish a sense of order amidst the noise and chaos, Captain Smith ducked into the wireless cabin. Junior Marconi operator Harold Bride was just getting out of bed to relieve the senior operator, Jack Phil-

A few minutes later Captain Smith put out a call for all passengers to go on deck. Many believed the call was just a matter of form, like a fire drill at school, nothing more. After all, they had noticed just a slight jar and had heard a little grinding noise. Some of the passengers had seen water on board but only in small amounts. There were no bells or alarms. Besides, they were on the *Titanic*, the unsinkable ship. No one seemed sure whether they should laugh, panic, or pray.

Even members of the crew were not certain how to react. In second and third class, stewards were throwing cabin doors open and telling everyone to get out of bed, put life jackets on, and get up to the Boat Deck. In first class, the stewards knocked on cabin doors to wake passengers. Some of them put their life jackets on over their fur coats. Others refused to go up on deck or even to unlock their cabin doors.

Several passengers helped break down a jammed door to free a man trapped behind it. After they did so, a steward came along and said he would have them all arrested for destroying the *Titanic*'s property when the ship arrived in New York.

Down in the engine room, Chief Engineer Joseph Bell and a few crewmen kept enough steam up so that the ship would have power to keep the lights burning and the pumps going.

Up on the Boat Deck, the crew was beginning to make progress with the lifeboats. There were sixteen wooden lifeboats in all, eight on either side of the ship. Each of these boats was built to hold up to sixty-five people. In addition, four collapsible canvas lifeboats, each

WHY THE HULL FILLED WITH WATER

Most experts believe that the iceberg ripped a 300-foot (90-meter) gash in the starboard side of the ship. Then water began pouring into the first six watertight sections of the hull. The electric doors between all sixteen sections were closed immediately, but the water continued to rise in the first six sections faster than the electric pumps could pump it out. The water in these sections rose higher and higher, until it finally began spilling over the bulkheads and filling the other sections one at a time.

with a much smaller passenger capacity, were also stored on the deck. To prepare the wooden boats, the crew had to remove their canvas covers, hitch the boats to the **davits**, swing the boats over the side of the deck, load them with passengers, and lower them 70 feet or so (21 meters) to the water. For a crew that had never practiced, it was a slow, complicated procedure.

Perhaps the most difficult task of all, however, was persuading passengers to board the lifeboats. It was so cold outside that many preferred to stay in the lounges and smoking rooms where it was warm and where it still seemed like a safe place to be. Many passengers were reluctant to get into the lifeboats because they thought the whole affair was silly. Why go out in a rowboat and float around in the cold sea for hours, only to come back to the ship in the morning? As John Jacob Astor put it: "We are safer here than in that little boat." The

few passengers who did board the first lifeboats were teased by the other passengers. "You'll need a pass to get back on," they said, and laughed.

In the first-class lounge, many passengers gathered while they weighed the pros and cons of boarding the lifeboats. Here bandmaster Wallace Hartley had assembled his eight-piece band. Playing a variety of ragtime tunes, the musicians did their best to keep the ship's party atmosphere alive.

All this time, water had continued pouring in below. As the bow of the ship tilted more deeply into the water, passengers on deck had to lean forward to work their way to the stern of the ship. Those trying to reach the Boat Deck found the stairs increasingly difficult to climb.

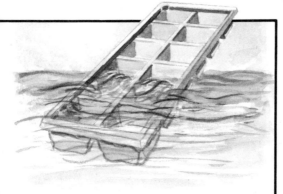

You can picture the hull filling with water if you place a plastic ice cube tray in water. When none of the sections of the tray contain water, it floats. If you slowly tip one end into the water, the tray will fill up one section at a time. When only one or two sections are filled, the tray will still float. But as more sections gradually fill with water, the weight pulls the whole tray under.

As the crew began lowering lifeboats from the davits, some people on board realized that the ship really was in danger. Strange as it may seem, one of the last to know of the danger was the lookout.

When Quartermaster Thomas Rowe relieved Fred Fleet in the crow's nest, Fleet told him about the iceberg gliding by. Forty minutes later, as he was looking out into the night for signs of danger, Rowe was surprised to see a lifeboat off the starboard side. He telephoned the bridge to ask if the ship's officers knew there was a lifeboat afloat. The officer who answered Rowe's call was amazed that no one had informed Rowe of the accident. Now Captain Smith ordered Rowe to come to the bridge at once and to bring some rockets, which were stored one deck below the crow's nest.

From the bridge of the *Titanic*, the lights of another ship were clearly visible on the northern horizon. Captain Smith hoped to attract the attention of its crew. At about 12:45 A.M., Rowe reached the bridge with a box of eight rockets. Smith immediately ordered that one be fired every few minutes. Visible for at least 20 miles (32.2 kilometers), the white rockets exploded like plain fireworks. White rockets were recognized in the shipping world as a signal of distress.

Within moments, the first rocket whistled and soared high above, then burst, releasing a shower of white sparks. Meanwhile, another officer tried contacting the unidentified ship with the *Titanic's* **Morse lamp**, and for a moment thought he was getting a response. He saw something flickering like a lamp on the other boat, but he could not make out a signal. It was just the ship's **mast** light flickering, he decided.

On the Boat Deck, the situation was growing more chaotic by the moment. While the crew had managed to lower the first few lifeboats successfully, hardly anyone had bothered to board them. Now people were scrambling to find a seat in one. As in any shipwreck, two rules applied: Women and children first; and the captain goes down with the ship. Husbands and wives were now parting, some tearfully, some quietly.

Many husbands were reassuring their wives. Dan Marvin, recently married, blew a kiss and told his bride, "It's all right, little girl. You go and I'll stay a while."

Others promised they would be on the next boat. Still, some wives refused to go. First-class passenger Arthur Ryerson spoke firmly to Mrs. Ryerson:

You must obey orders. When they say "Women and children to the boats," you must go when your turn comes. I'll stay here. I'll be all right.

No one, however, could persuade Mrs. Isidor Straus. "I've always stayed with my husband. Why should I leave him now?" she said.

At one point, she even crossed the Boat Deck and almost stepped into lifeboat No. 8. But then she returned to her husband.

"We've been living together for so many years," she said. "Where you go I go."

John Jacob Astor was about to follow his young, pregnant wife, Madeleine, onto a lifeboat when one of the crew told him the boat was for women and chil-

dren only. Meekly, the richest man on board stepped back.

Benjamin Guggenheim reportedly went to his cabin with his valet, and both returned in their finest evening clothes. As Guggenheim explained to a steward:

I think there is grave doubt that the men will get off. I am willing to remain and play the man's game if there are not enough boats for more than the women and children. Tell my wife…I played the game out straight and to the end. No woman shall be left aboard this ship because Ben Guggenheim was a coward.

J. Bruce Ismay had been helping lower the lifeboats as if he were a member of the crew. Unlike the crew members, however, who were expected to stay with the captain until he released them, Ismay climbed into one of the lifeboats as it was being lowered.

The stern of the ship was soon tipping up out of the water and the bow was submerged. Water covered the **forecastle** and swirled around the foot of the mast.

The crowd on the Boat Deck was growing larger and more uncontrollable. Stewards had unlocked the steerage gates, and people from third class began to make their way up to the Boat Deck. They rushed madly for the few remaining lifeboats. Almost all of the women and children from first and second class had been put on lifeboats. But many third-class women and children remained on board, and there was little room for them in the lifeboats.

As lifeboat No. 14 was being loaded, a throng of passengers advanced on the boat, and a crewman had to hold them off with the boat's **tiller**. When another group began closing in, Fifth Officer Lowe pulled out a pistol.

"If anyone else tries that, this is what he'll get!" he shouted, as he fired three shots into the air.

As they held off the unruly mob, the crew continued lowering the lifeboats. At 1:55 A.M., they finished loading No. 4, the last wooden lifeboat, and lowered it into the water. Normally the Boat Deck was 70 feet (21 meters) above the water. Now crew members were shocked to find that they had to lower lifeboats only about 15 feet (4.5 meters) to the water.

With about 1,500 passengers still on board, only three canvas collapsible lifeboats remained. Each one was capable of holding forty-seven people, and only one of them was fully opened and ready to lower into the water. Fending off the crowd, the crew locked hands around this last open lifeboat, letting only women and children through.

Then, as they began to lower the boat over the side, one of the first-class passengers, Colonel Archibald Gracie, rushed forward with two women he had befriended on the trip, Miss Edith Evans and Mrs. John Murray Brown. He watched as the two women passed through the line of crewmen and toward the boat. The boat was already over the side and almost beyond reach, so Miss Evans helped Mrs. Brown over the rail saying, "You go first, you have children." Then the boat was quickly lowered away with forty-four people on board. Mrs. Brown was among them, but Miss Evans was not.

THE *TITANIC* SIGNALS FOR HELP

The crew of the *Titanic* used every available means of communication to call for help. The most effective was the Marconi, or wireless, telegraph machine (1). This machine, invented in 1895, was an early form of radio that transmitted telegraph signals through the air.

The *Titanic's* wireless was a powerful instrument, and its calls for help were received by ships as far as 500 miles away (800 kilometers). But the ship closest to the *Titanic*, sitting just 20 miles (32 kilometers) to the north, did not receive any of these messages.

The *Titanic's* crew also tried to send an SOS signal to this ship using a Morse lamp (2). But apparently no one saw the signal. Finally, the Titanic sent up eight white flares (3), recognized internationally as a signal of distress. These, too, were unheeded by the nearby ship.

At 2:05 A.M., Captain Smith came into the wireless cabin again. Phillips had his life jacket on but was still sending out the distress signal. Bride was standing by. They had managed to contact several ships, including the *Titanic's* sister ship the *Olympic*. But she was 500 miles away (805 kilometers).

Unfortunately, they had received no response from the ship that had been spotted earlier, less than 20 miles away (32.2 kilometers). The nearest ship they had contacted was the *Carpathia*, which was 58 miles (93 kilometers) to the southeast. Captained by Arthur Rostron, it was now heading full steam for the *Titanic*.

Captain Smith felt it was time to dismiss his crew. He told the wireless operators:

Men you have done your full duty. You can do no more. Abandon your cabin. Now it's every man for himself.

Then Bride and Phillips left the wireless cabin and went out on deck. Clad in life jackets, the band stood on deck near the grand staircase and played on. All the wooden lifeboats had been lowered, but two collapsibles remained stowed on the roof of the officer's quarters. Several crew members were trying to cut the ropes that held the collapsibles in place and wrestle the bulky, canvas boats over the side of the ship. They succeeded in getting one of the boats to the side railing. But there seemed to be no way to get it over the railing and into the water.

On the opposite side of the ship, crew members were having the same problem with the other collapsible. Colonel Gracie, had loaned them his penknife to cut the ropes. They had eased the boat down off the roof. But pushing it up the severely slanting deck was impossible.

At 2:15 A.M., while the men on board struggled with the collapsibles, the bow slid further under water, and a great wave came rolling over the Boat Deck. Those on deck scrambled toward the stern. There they were met by a mass of third-class passengers just coming up from lower decks.

The band, which had been playing ragtime all night, switched to a somber, soothing hymn called "Autumn." The music ended quickly, since the band members could not keep their footing. The *Titanic's* lights flickered off once, came back on, then went out forever.

Colonel Gracie, who was still on the ship, recalled the scene:

The submerged forecastle was now beginning to shudder, shaking very much as the sea poured into A and B Decks, flooding the first-class quarters, the lounges and the saloons. The impending crisis jolted everyone still aboard the ship.

At the stern of the ship, people grabbed onto the railings, fighting to keep from sliding on the deck, which was slanting more steeply by the moment.

Seventeen-year-old Jack Thayer Jr. and his newfound friend Milton Long were by the starboard rail, near the second smokestack, trying to stay clear of the crowd that had come up from below. The water was about 10 feet (3 meters) below the deck when they decided to jump. Long was hanging onto the railing and facing the ship. He let go and dropped into the water. Thayer sat on the railing ten more seconds, then jumped as far as he could. Thayer found his way to safety. Long didn't.

As it swept over the deck, seawater caught both of the collapsible lifeboats and threw them overboard. The forward smokestack crashed into the water, creating a wave that pushed one collapsible clear of the wreckage. On the Boat Deck, Colonel Gracie jumped in the path of a wave and bodysurfed toward the stern, where he grabbed a railing and held on for his life. He hung on as the stern kept rising straight into the air.

It hovered motionlessly in the air, the three propellers idle and dripping. Inside, dishware, furniture, cargo, and machinery plunged toward the bow. The noise was incredible, as survivor Lawrence Beesley remembered:

> It was partly a roar, partly a groan, partly a rattle, and partly a smash, and it was not a sudden roar as an explosion would be; it went on successively for some seconds, possibly fifteen to twenty, as the heavy machinery dropped down to the... bow of the ship.... But it was a noise no one had heard before, and no one wishes to hear again: it was stupefying, stupendous, as it came to us along the water.

Finally, the terrific noise subsided. The stern glided down at a slant, picking up speed as she did so, until she quietly gurgled under, leaving the sea above it calm and flat. When the ship went under, Colonel Gracie still hung onto the railing and the sea rushed in. At the last minute, he realized he had better abandon ship:

> I was hanging on to that railing, but I soon let go.... When I came up to the surface there was no ship there.... All around me was wreckage.

The *Titanic* had sunk.

Five
Help Arrives

No one knows exactly what happened to all the people who were still on board when the *Titanic* finally **foundered**. Hundreds of people jumped into the freezing water, and hundreds more were stuck inside the ship. Some may have been crushed by falling debris, while many others quickly succumbed to the icy cold.

At 28 degrees Fahrenheit (-2 degrees Celsius), the water was well below freezing. Swimmers tried to reach whatever they thought they could hang on to. Nearby, deck chairs and other debris floated by along with the two collapsibles. One was half full of water. The other was upside down. This collapsible was the closest lifeboat to the *Titanic* when the ship went under and was nearly crushed by the smokestack that toppled over before the ship submerged.

The wave created by the smokestack pushed the collapsible clear of the ship though, and soon people were crawling on board. One by one, those who were near enough and strong enough climbed on the boat.

After a while, Colonel Gracie appeared alongside and hoisted himself on. Bride came out from underneath the collapsible and pulled himself on. Before long, thirty men were sitting or lying on the upside-down boat, and it began to sag beneath them. They knew that if they took on any more weight, the boat might sink. So a few of the men used planks to paddle away from those still in the water, as others fended off the swimmers who tried to get on board.

The night air was filled with cries for help and the sounds of people thrashing about in the freezing water. Fifth Officer Lowe managed to locate four partially empty lifeboats about 150 yards (136 meters) away from where the *Titanic* had been. He tied these boats together, divided his passengers among them, and went back in his boat to look for survivors.

By the time he reached the spot where the *Titanic* had gone down, it was nearly 3:00 A.M. He heard only an occasional cry, and when he was able to chase it down, he was usually too late. In spite of this brave effort, Lowe could rescue only four passengers, and one died within the hour. Although several of the wooden lifeboats were partially empty, only Lowe's boat returned to the scene.

When the *Titanic* went under, most of the lifeboats were within about 300 yards (273 meters) and had room for additional passengers. No. 1, which could hold forty people, had only twelve on board. Yet when fireman Charles Hendrickson said twice, "It's time for us to go back and pick up anyone in the water," Sir Cosmo Duff Gordon was the only one who responded. He thought it was a bad idea. So they decided to row away from the *Titanic*.

Soon it made no difference. A person could not live long in water so cold.

The distant shouts became fewer, then died away completely.

Now Jean Gertrude Hippach, in boat No. 4, looked up in the clear night sky and saw shooting stars, more than she had ever seen before. She remembered hearing once that every shooting star means someone has died.

Among the most notable passengers who did not survive was John Jacob Astor. His frozen body was found a few days later. Thomas Andrews, the designer of the ship, did not survive. Wireless operator Harold Bride survived, but his co-worker Jack Phillips did not. Mr. and Mrs. Straus were last seen huddled together in a deck chair on board. None of the eight members of the Goodwin family was ever found.

Millionairess Molly Brown was in boat No. 6, commanded by Quartermaster Robert Hitchens. Hitchens had cursed the women in his boat and ordered them to row faster, even though he refused to row himself. Brown succeeded in taking over command of the boat, and became known thereafter as "the unsinkable Molly Brown."

WHAT HAPPENED TO CAPTAIN SMITH?

Several stories about the fate of Captain E.J. Smith have survived. Some passengers claimed to have seen the stately commander shoot himself just before the ship went under. But Harold Bride said that he saw the captain dive off the bridge into the sea. Others placed him in the water afterwards, rescuing a baby and swimming up to a lifeboat. Someone reportedly pulled him into the boat, but he slipped back into the water, saying, "Goodbye boys, I'm going to follow the ship."

The exact circumstances of his death will never be known. What is certain is that Captain Smith was one of the 1,522 who died in the North Atlantic that night.

Through the night, people tried desperately to stay warm and wondered how long they might drift in the icy waters. In all the boats, people tried to remain optimistic as they waited for someone to rescue them. They took turns rowing, and some people prayed. Fourth Officer Joseph Boxhall had some green flares, which he fired periodically from boat No. 2. This seemed to cheer people up as they waited for dawn and hoped for a rescue ship.

Meanwhile, the *Carpathia* was on her way. She carried 150 first-class passengers, mostly American retirees, on what had started as a warm-weather cruise from New York to Gibraltar. She was about 58 miles (93 kilometers) southeast of the *Titanic* when the unbelievable distress signal came across her wireless. Several of the *Carpathia's* passengers awoke in the early morning hours of April 15 to unexpectedly cold

Captain Arthur Rostron of the *Carpathia*

cabins and the roar of the ship's engines going full steam as they headed north.

Captain Arthur Rostron had been asleep when the *Titanic's* distress call came at around 1:00 A.M. Awakened by the *Carpathia's* wireless operator, he immediately changed the ship's course and cut off all heat and hot water, putting all the steam into the engines. During the top-speed run, he put the crew to work organizing for the emergency. They hauled out extra blankets, swung out all the lifeboats, opened all the gangway doors, rigged cargo nets to help people up the side, and prepared the ship's cranes to hoist any luggage aboard.

Although her normal cruising speed was much slower, with all available hands shoveling coal into the boilers, Captain Rostron was able to bring the *Carpathia* up to a shaky seventeen knots.

By 4:00 A.M., the *Carpathia* was there. Rostron stopped the engines and looked around. The ship had been firing rockets every fifteen minutes as they approached the area to let any survivors know that help was on the way. Now her crew peered into the darkness and saw nothing. Then someone spotted a green flare – Fourth Officer Boxhall's last one – about 300 yards away (275 meters). Still dodging icebergs, the captain maneuvered the *Carpathia* toward the lifeboat. Finally, at 4:10 A.M., the first *Titanic* passenger climbed up the swinging ladder and onto the *Carpathia*. When Boxhall came on board, Captain Rostron sent for him and asked him the question to which he already knew the answer: "The *Titanic* has gone down?"

"Yes," said Boxhall, his voice breaking. "She went down at about 2:30 A.M."

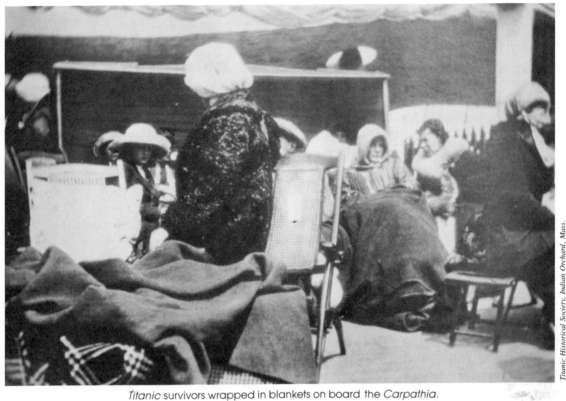

Titanic survivors wrapped in blankets on board the *Carpathia*.

Spread out over 4 miles (6.4 kilometers), the other lifeboats were not easy to spot in the dark. As the cold night gave way to dawn, the shivering passengers on the lifeboats were greeted by an eerie sight. They were surrounded by dozens of small icebergs and three or four huge ones, rising 150 to 200 feet (45 to 60 meters) out of the water.

As if in a maze, the crew of the *Carpathia* searched among the icebergs for the remaining lifeboats. Lifeboats would appear for a moment, then disappear behind an iceberg. Northwest of the *Carpathia*, about 5 miles (8 kilometers) away, one could see a flat, continuous ice field, with a few of the giant bergs pointing up into the sky. It stretched as far as the eye could see.

By sunrise, all the survivors from the *Titanic* had been rescued. In the brisk morning air, the *Carpathia's* crew threw warm blankets over the new guests. As they came on board, they were welcomed with hot coffee, cocoa, and brandy. Hardly anyone spoke. The loss of family and friends and the ordeal the survivors had been through seemed too much for words.

J. Bruce Ismay, who had helped decide that the *Titanic* should carry fewer lifeboats, identified himself when he came aboard. But he refused to go to the dining room with everyone else. Instead, the *Carpathia's* doctor put Ismay in his room and decided it was best to keep him under sedation until they reached the next port.

By about 8:30 A.M., Captain Rostron decided there could not possibly be anyone left alive in the water and that it was time to go. Before he left, he summoned Reverend Anderson, one of his passengers, who conducted a brief memorial service in the main lounge.

As the *Carpathia* floated over the *Titanic's* final resting place, her passengers joined with the *Titanic's* survivors in remembering the dead and gave thanks for the living. Just as the *Carpathia* was leaving with her flag at half-mast, a curious thing happened. Another small steamship, called the *Californian*, arrived.

The *Californian* was the unidentified ship that the crew of the *Titanic* had seen less than 20 miles away (32 kilometers). The *Titanic* had been unable to contact the *Californian* in spite of the crew's repeated efforts. If the smaller vessel had responded, the sinking of the *Titanic* might have been much less tragic.

As it steamed into view seven hours too late, however, the *Californian* was just another lost opportunity to save the lives of those who drowned. Why she did not respond earlier remains a mystery to this day.

About the time the *Carpathia* was leaving the scene of the disaster, newspapers in New York were putting together their first editions of the day. Relying on their wireless machines, the only solid news they had about the disaster was that the *Titanic* had sent two messages. First, it had reported hitting an iceberg and was asking for help. A second message said that the bow was flooded and women were being put in lifeboats. At White Star offices in New

York, reporters were clamoring for a quote from company vice president Phillip A.S. Franklin. He gave them one:

We place absolute confidence in the Titanic. *We believe that the boat is unsinkable.*

Most of the reporters believed him. "ALL SAVED FROM *TITANIC* AFTER COLLISION," blared the April 15 *New York Sun*. The *Wall Street Journal* had this to say about the "near-disaster:"

The gravity of the damage to the Titanic *is apparent, but the important point is that she did not sink. Her watertight bulkheads were really watertight.*

Only *The New York Times* went out on a limb. Managing Editor Carr Van Anda guessed that the *Titanic's* silence after those first two ominous messages spelled the ship's doom. The paper's

A STRANGE COINCIDENCE

In 1898, fourteen years before the *Titanic's* maiden voyage, an author named Morgan Robertson wrote a novel called *Futility*. The book was about a huge and wonderful ship, bigger than any that had ever been built. In Robertson's book, the ship was filled with rich and famous people. Tragically, it hit an iceberg and went down on a cold April night.

Robertson's boat was 800 feet long (244 meters); the *Titanic* was 882 feet long (269 meters). Both had triple screw propellers, and could go as fast as 20 to 25 knots. Both could carry about 3,000 people, and had lifeboats for far less. Both were called unsinkable.

Robertson's ship was called the *Titan*!

early edition reported that women and children were being put on the lifeboats. The late edition reported that the *Titanic* had sunk.

With conflicting reports in the newspapers and rumors circulating in the streets, it was hard for anyone to learn the facts. But the White Star office was swamped with thousands of inquiries about the *Titanic's* passengers. Family and friends wanted to know what had happened.

The only way to get more informa-

tion was by wireless, but the *Carpathia's* wireless could send messages only 200 miles (322 kilometers). Finally, the *Carpathia* was able to send a list of survivors to the *Olympic*, which was within its range. The *Olympic* then used its more powerful Marconi machine to send the list on to New York.

In New York, one of the most powerful Marconi machines was at Wanamaker's Department Store. On April 15, at 4:35 P.M., David Sarnoff was operating the Wanamaker's wireless when he caught a signal from the *Olympic*. From 1,400 miles (2,254 kilometers) out at sea, the message came: The *Titanic* had sunk at 12:47 A.M. New York time, and her only known survivors, about 675 people, were headed for New York aboard the *Carpathia*.

At first the news was received with shock and disbelief, then with grief and outrage. The *Titanic* had sunk. More than 1,500 people, including several leaders of American industry, were dead. People wept in the streets of New York and around the world.

Crowds of people outside the offices of White Star Lines in New York await news about the Titanic's passengers.

Titanic Historical Society, Indian Orchard, Mass.

WHY DIDN'T THE *CALIFORNIAN* RESPOND?

If help had arrived before the *Titanic* sank, hundreds of lives—perhaps all lives—could have been saved. The only ship close enough to reach the *Titanic* in time was the *Californian*.

A relatively slow, small liner with room for 47 passengers, the steamship *Californian* was traveling from London to Boston. She carried no passengers this trip, which had so far been uneventful. Sunday, April 14, had been a long day for the ship's crew, and Captain Stanley Lord had decided to stop for the night rather than continue steaming into icy waters. The ship stopped less than 20 miles (32.2 kilometers) from the *Titanic*.

Cyril Evans, the wireless operator on board the *Californian*, had shut down at 11:30 P.M., his normal quitting time. Just half an hour earlier, Evans had sent a warning to the *Titanic* about ice in the immediate area.

At that moment in the *Titanic's* wireless cabin, Jack Phillips was working feverishly, sending a pile of personal messages for the passengers. When the nearby *Californian* burst in, its signal came across loud and clear, "Say, Old Man, we are stopped and surrounded by ice."

The message was so loud, in fact, that Phillips felt like it nearly broke his eardrums. Irritated, he told the *Californian*: "Shut up, shut up, I am busy."

At about that same time, on the *Californian's* bridge, Third Officer Charles Groves noticed a ship steaming along about 20 miles (32.2 kilometers) to the south. Judging by the bright lights on deck, he figured it had to be a big passenger ship. He watched it for about twenty minutes as it continued moving at a rapid pace. Groves knew there was drifting ice in the area, so at about 11:30 P.M. he went to the chart room and told Captain Lord about the big ship off in the distance.

"That will be the *Titanic* on her maiden voyage," said Captain Lord.

He told Groves to try to contact the ship by Morse lamp. As Groves returned to the bridge and prepared to do so, he saw the ship stop. It then seemed to turn out many of its lights. Groves, an experienced seaman, had seen other ships turn out their lights at midnight to encourage passengers to go to bed, so he wasn't surprised.

What he didn't know was that the *Titanic's* lights had not gone out. The ship had just turned sharply to port, changing his view of its well-lit deck. Groves signaled with his Morse lamp anyway, but received no response.

At midnight, Groves finished his watch and stopped at the wireless cabin to visit Evans, who was reading a magazine and did not feel much like talking. Groves put on the headphones from the wireless machine for a few minutes. Since the machine did not seem to be working, he removed the headphones and left. At about 12:15 A.M., Jack Phillips sent out the *Titanic's* signal of distress.

At about the same time, Second Officer Herbert Stone was standing on the *Californian's* deck when he was surprised by the sight of an exploding rocket from a nearby ship.

"Strange that a ship would be firing rockets," he thought. It wasn't every night that you saw those.

In the next ten minutes, he and apprentice James Gibson counted four more rockets, then another at 1:00 A.M. and still another at 1:05 A.M. Finally, at about 1:10 A.M., Stone went to the chart room and told Captain Lord about the rockets.

"Are they company signals?" asked the captain.

"I don't know," the second officer replied. "But they appear to me to be white rockets."

Apparently, Captain Lord did not connect the rockets with the ship he had identified earlier as the *Titanic*. Now the captain told Stone to try signalling this ship with a Morse lamp. Then he went to his cabin to go to sleep.

Stone relayed the captain's order to apprentice Gibson, and had him try a second time to contact the ship with the Morse lamp. Gibson once thought he was getting a response, and asked for Stone's binoculars to take a closer look.

"No," Gibson told the second officer. "It was just the ship's mast light flickering." Then, with the glasses still to his eyes, he saw another rocket, the sixth. Perhaps it was a celebration of some sort, he thought.

Second Officer Stone and apprentice Gibson saw two more rockets around 1:50 A.M. Stone watched the ship with his binoculars. After a while he remarked to Gibson:

"Have a look at her now. She looks very queer out of the water. Her lights look queer." Gibson took a look, and remarked that the ship looked as if it had "a big side out of the water."

By 2:15 A.M., Gibson and Stone had seen a total of eight rockets fired. All were white, the internationally recognized distress signal. Then the ship disappeared from view into the southwest. They woke Captain Lord to tell him. He asked if any of the rockets had colors in them.

"No," said Gibson. "They were all white." After asking what time it was, the captain went back to sleep. It was 2:20 A.M.

At about 5:40 A.M., an uneasy crew member woke wireless operator Evans to see if he could find out anything more about the ship that had been firing rockets during the night. The lookout claimed he had seen more rockets a few hours later, but he thought they came from another ship. Evans turned on his machine, put on the headphones, and heard from another ship that the *Titanic* had hit an iceberg and sunk. The crewman raced up to tell Captain Lord, who immediately made the order to begin steaming toward the *Titanic's* last reported position. His order came about seven hours too late.

Six
She Lives On

Ever since that cold April night in 1912, the world has been fascinated by the story of the "unsinkable" *Titanic*. The accounts of the incident told by surviving passengers are as dramatic as any story in history. Yet many questions remain unanswered: Why did the *Titanic* sink? Could the disaster have been avoided? Could more lives have been saved?

We will never know exactly what happened that night. Immediately after the shipwreck, however, both the American and British governments launched formal investigations to try to find out. Although their conclusions differed in many respects, they agreed on one particular count. Both investigations found fault with Captain Lord of the *Californian*.

They concluded that the crew of the *Californian* saw eight rockets. Even though Lord was informed of this, he neglected to respond. Further, the *Californian* made no attempt to inquire about the condition of the nearby ship

by wireless. Finally, two of the crew members on watch that night felt there was cause for concern, and Captain Lord failed to act.

The British investigation was conducted by the Board of Trade, the agency responsible for safety regulations aboard British ships. They found that Captain Smith, the captain of the *Titanic*, had followed standard procedures and had acted professionally. And Lord Mersey, who headed the investigation, believed that they should not be too hard on a man who was not there to defend himself.

The American investigation, headed by Michigan Senator William Smith, placed final responsibility for the tragedy firmly on the White Star Line and the carelessness of Captain Smith. Specifically, the investigation concluded that the *Titanic* was not prepared for an emergency. The crew had

COULD THE COLLISION HAVE BEEN AVOIDED?

The sinking of the *Titanic* resulted from an unlikely series of events. The collision with the iceberg should never have happened, and here are a few reasons why:

1. The Titanic *received six ice warnings*. But no single person on board, including Captain Smith, ever saw all six warnings of icebergs in the area.

2. The ship was going too fast. Although it was dark out and the ship was in an area known to have icebergs, Captain Smith had the *Titanic* running nearly full speed.

3. The captain and crew were poorly prepared for an emergency. Before her maiden voyage, the *Titanic* had never undergone thorough trials. No one knew how quickly she turned, or how long it took her to stop.

4. Captain Smith was overconfident. Although he had received several ice warnings, Captain Smith did not order a special lookout. Nor did he stay at the bridge as the *Titanic* entered the area where icebergs had been reported.

not even been drilled in loading and lowering the lifeboats.

In addition, the *Titanic* had received repeated ice warnings and indications that other ships had taken the precaution of stopping for the night. Yet Captain Smith did not even slow down. Nor did he take his position on the bridge when the *Titanic* entered the area where icebergs had been spotted. He ordered no special lookout. There was not even a pair of binoculars in the crow's nest.

In his address to the U.S. Senate on May 12, 1912, Senator Smith said of the captain:

> *His indifference to danger was one of the direct...causes of this unnecessary tragedy, while his own willingness to die was... evidence of his fitness to live. Those of us who knew him well, not in anger but in sorrow, file one specific charge against him: overconfidence and neglect to heed the oft-repeated warnings of his friends.*

In spite of their differences, the American and British investigations led to reforms in the shipping business. In the United States, legislation introduced by Senator Smith resulted in the formation of the International Ice Patrol. It still operates, keeping a constant count of icebergs and reporting their locations to nearby ships.

Also, ever since the sinking of the *Titanic*, it has been required by law that every ship at sea have a radio operator on duty twenty-four hours a day. The operators must keep track of all communications and report navigation warnings to the crew. British and American shipping regulations were also changed to insure that every ship has enough lifeboats for all passengers and crew members.

The *Titanic* had hardly settled on the bottom of the Atlantic before people began talking about finding her and bringing her back up. In 1914, Charles Smith of Denver came up with a plan to rig a submarine with electromagnets and haul the ship to the surface. Over the years, others planned to bring the *Titanic* up by filling it with floating materials, such as molten wax, Ping-Pong balls, petroleum jelly, and, ironically, ice.

It was not until 1981, however, that the technology was available to explore the ocean floor scientifically. Then a team of oceanographers, funded by Texas oilman Jack Grimm, worked through the summers of 1981 and 1982 using **sonar** to chart the ocean floor near the *Titanic's* last reported position. Even with their sophisticated equipment, they were unable to locate the wreck. Frustrated, they finally quit the expensive search.

Like many others who dreamed of finding and raising her, Robert D. Ballard had been intrigued by the story of the *Titanic* since his childhood. He had always been interested in the sea. As he studied to become a marine biologist, Ballard came to believe that the technical and professional demands of finding the *Titanic* made it the ultimate challenge.

In 1973, Ballard began giving the idea more serious consideration. He was a member of the Alvin Group, a team of oceanographers at the Woods Hole Oceanographic Institute in Woods Hole, Massachusetts. The Alvin Group worked with *Alvin*, a small, three-person submarine named after one of its developers, Al Vine. A new **titanium** steel alloy had recently made it possible for *Alvin* to descend twice as far as it could with its old, steel hull.

To Ballard and other oceanographers, this was an exciting technological advance. With *Alvin*, they could go to the deepest parts of the ocean and see things they had never seen before. Ballard also knew that this new piece of technology could help him achieve his lifelong dream of finding the *Titanic*.

Although taking up the search would be expensive, Ballard believed that such an expedition would be worth the cost. It would not only answer questions about the *Titanic*, but it would have other benefits as well. The high-tech methods developed by the search would help marine biologists find out more about life on the ocean floor.

For several years Ballard tried to raise money for the Titanic expedition. He suffered many setbacks, including the loss of six hundred thousand dollars worth of borrowed deep-sea search equipment in an accident at sea. But he also worked with the National Geographic Society, which became extremely interested in his project.

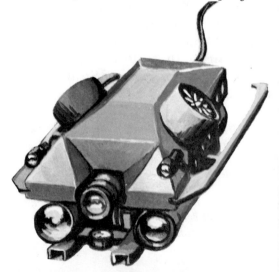

LOOKING FOR THE *TITANIC*

The search for the *Titanic* led to the development of *Argo*, an unmanned deep-sea **submersible**. Connected to a mother ship by a long cable, *Argo* was equipped with remote-control lights, two sonar systems, and five video cameras. Both of *Argo's* sonar systems and one on the mother ship sent sound waves in a variety of directions. These sound waves echoed, or bounced, off the ocean floor. Instruments on board the mother ship could determine the size and shape of objects struck by the sound waves. Whenever they revealed anything of interest, it could be viewed through *Argo's* video cameras.

And researchers from the Society helped develop underwater color video cameras that would help him later.

In 1985, with the backing of the National Geographic Society, Ballard and his crew finally took up the search. They had developed an unmanned deep-sea **submersible** named *Argo* that combined sonar and video technology.

Ballard's research team began the search in July, joining forces with a team of French scientists led by Jean-Louis Michel on the French research vessel *Le Suroit*. In August, they continued the search on board a new American research ship, the *Knorr*. Working in shifts, the scientists sat day and night in the control room monitoring their sonar equipment and staring into the video screens. All they saw was the mud on the ocean floor.

Finally, on August 31, 1985, at about 1:15 A.M., approximately 10 miles (16.1 kilometers) from the *Titanic's* last reported position, crewmen Bill Lange and Stu Harris spotted pieces of wreckāge on their video screens. At first they saw only bits of debris. They were unrecognizable, but seemed to be man-made. Then, at a depth of 2.5 miles (4 kilometers) below the surface, one of the *Titanic's* huge boilers came into view.

52

At first they could hardly believe it, but then Lieutenant George Rey reported that he had something on the sonar. Soon the control room was alive with activity. Someone told Ballard the good news: They had found at least a piece of the *Titanic's* wreckage. At last it was confirmed—they had located the ship.

The crew was jubilant, but as the clock edged toward 2:00 A.M., they became quiet. They remembered what had brought them there, and a feeling of sadness crept into their excitement. At 2:20 A.M., the same time the *Titanic* had sunk, Ballard and some of the others on board gathered at the stern of the *Knorr*.

They raised the flag of Harland & Wolff, the shipyards where the *Titanic* had been built, and observed a few moments of silence. It was quiet and calm, like that night seventy-three years earlier. Those on board the *Knorr* pictured the *Titanic* as she was that night, her bow sinking fast and her stern rising straight up. They imagined the lifeboats and the desperate cries for help from hundreds of people freezing to death in the cold waters.

As soon as those brief moments of silence were over, the crew went back to work. Over the next four days, the *Knorr*

swept back and forth over the wreck, towing *Argo* far below. The crew collected the best pictures they could before heading home to Woods Hole.

The next summer they returned to the site, this time with *Alvin*, the three-person submarine, and *Jason*, its **robotic** underwater camera. Now they

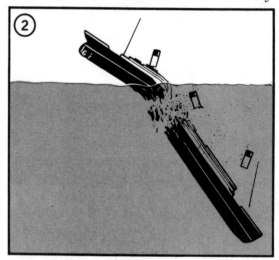

could get up close with the submarine, and *Jason* could explore parts of the ship where even the submarine could not go. Ballard and the members of his crew put their new high-tech tools to use and thoroughly documented the scene of the wreck. It took nine trips to the *Titanic* to do the job, diving 2.5 miles (4 kilometers) to the ocean floor each time. In all, they took seventy thousand still pictures and miles of videotape.

They looked at the bow for the fatal gash from the iceberg, but the hull was buried too deeply in mud to see any scar. Ballard speculates that perhaps the iceberg made no gash at all. It is quite possible, he maintains, that the steel plates bent, but held, and the rivets popped, allowing the sea to pour in. In fact, Ballard found a horizontal buckling in the steel plates of the hull and a few rivets missing along the seam of two plates.

One issue was resolved conclusively by the Ballard expedition. From eyewitness accounts, it had never been clear whether the *Titanic* remained intact or had broken in two. We now know that the *Titanic* went down in two pieces. The expedition discovered the two sections resting on the ocean floor about 600 yards apart (546 meters), with much of the ship's debris scattered between them.

The crew knew that the ship could never be raised in this condition. But they were able to explore it and photograph it so that others could see it. The findings from this expedition have allowed us to picture the *Titanic's* final moments more clearly than ever.

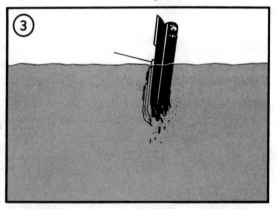

As the bow of the ship filled with water, it began to nose heavily downward. Finally the weight of the bow became too much, and at about 2:15 A.M., the ship was torn in two, ripping apart near the third smokestack—probably the weakest portion of the hull, where an expansion joint had been built in.

By the time the bow tore away, most of the remaining passengers on board had already clambered back to the stern. Undamaged until then, the stern now leveled off for a minute or two. As the water rushed in, the stern, too, began to tip forward, until the tail end of the boat was sticking straight up in the air. People clung together and hung onto anything they could, until they dropped into the freezing water below. It took only another minute or two for the stern portion to fill with water and submerge, carrying any passengers still on board to their deaths at the bottom of the ocean.

THE FINAL PLUNGE

1. At about 2:17 A.M., the flooding increased dramatically and the bow of the ship lurched downward. The first smokestack collapsed, as did the bridge and forward officers' quarters. A few minutes later, the second smokestack collapsed.

2. Approximately fifteen minutes later, amid terrible noise, witnesses recalled seeing the stern level itself momentarily. This was almost certainly the moment that the hull broke in two.

3. While the bow sank slowly to the bottom, the stern stood straight up in the air. Remarkably, it turned 180 degrees and remained in this position for about two minutes.

4. Finally, at approximately 2:47 A.M., the stern went under. It fell rapidly, end-over-end, and crashed on the ocean floor about 2,000 feet (600 meters) from the bow.

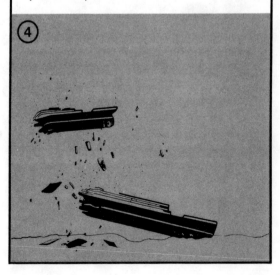

From the way it settled in the mud far below, Ballard determined that the bow fluttered down and landed softly. The stern portion landed much harder, however. Because it filled with water much faster, it sank faster, perhaps falling end over end, until it crash-landed on the ocean floor. When it hit, the ship's decks collapsed like a huge accordion.

Since she landed on the ocean floor that night, the *Titanic* has been home to the iron-eating bacteria that create rust. Now the rust flows in stream-like formations over nearly every steel surface of the ship. Almost all of her beautiful woodwork, except a few **teak** pillars near the grand staircase, has been eaten away.

There are only scattered clues about the passengers who were still on the ship when it sank. Several pairs of leather shoes sit on the bottom, lying as if there were feet still in them, in exactly the same position as when they fell there many years ago. One can almost imagine the scene of drowned passengers. But their bodies have long since disappeared, totally broken down by deep sea organisms. The ghostly white ceramic head of a child's doll also rests in the wreckage, the doll's body and clothing long gone.

Ballard and his crew also explored the Boat Deck, taking care not to get the

miniature submarine or its roving camera caught in the tangle of wires and twisted metal. They saw the spot where passengers had gathered to wait to get on the lifeboats and where the band had played until the end. In a field of debris near the wreck, they found many items swept off the decks by the deep sea currents. Tons of coal now litter the ocean floor. Cups, plates, floor tiles, suitcases, electric heaters, and chamber pots are scattered about. There are bottles of wine and champagne, many with corks still in them, perhaps still drinkable.

The opulence and majesty of the *Titanic* were short-lived. After three years of painstaking work to build her,

she was in active service for only four days. The story of the *Titanic* will live on for years, however, while the once-majestic ship lies peacefully at the bottom of the sea. Robert Ballard, the man responsible for finally discovering her, writes of the *Titanic's* undersea home:

> *The bottom of the ocean is a quiet place, a peaceful place, fitting for a memorial to all the things that sank when the* Titanic *went down. The wreck we found and photographed can stand as a monument to a mistake of arrogance, to a lost age, and to a kind of innocence we can't recover—and to the people, both guilty perpetrators and innocent victims, who figured in the drama.*

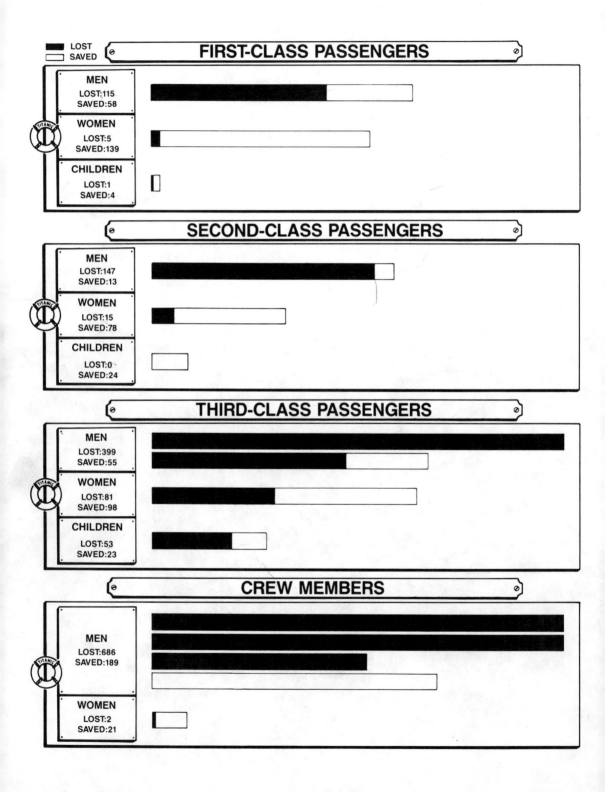

LOST
SAVED

FIRST-CLASS PASSENGERS

MEN
LOST:115
SAVED:58

WOMEN
LOST:5
SAVED:139

CHILDREN
LOST:1
SAVED:4

SECOND-CLASS PASSENGERS

MEN
LOST:147
SAVED:13

WOMEN
LOST:15
SAVED:78

CHILDREN
LOST:0
SAVED:24

THIRD-CLASS PASSENGERS

MEN
LOST:399
SAVED:55

WOMEN
LOST:81
SAVED:98

CHILDREN
LOST:53
SAVED:23

CREW MEMBERS

MEN
LOST:686
SAVED:189

WOMEN
LOST:2
SAVED:21

Epilogue

Two and a half miles below the surface of the Atlantic, the *Titanic's* torn and rusting hull rests in the mud on the ocean floor. It still seems incredible that even as she was going down, many people on board believed she was unsinkable. To this day, she is a symbol of overconfidence, ignored warnings, and tragic failure.

For many people, the incident marked the end of an era when life seemed simpler. Years later, Jack Thayer, who was a passenger on the *Titanic*, wrote of the disaster:

> The event . . . not only made the world rub its eyes and awake, but woke it with a start, keeping it moving at a rapidly accelerating pace ever since, with less and less peace, satisfaction and happiness. . . . To my mind, the world of today awoke April 15, 1912.

Thayer's father was one of the 1,522 passengers who died aboard the *Titanic*. So it is easy to understand why this was such a dominant event in Jack Thayer's life. But many others who were not as close to the disaster as Thayer also felt a great sense of loss.

Other disasters in other times have made people feel much the same way. For instance, when the space shuttle *Challenger* exploded on January 28, 1986, killing all seven astronauts on board, people around the world were shocked and saddened by the event. Like the *Titanic*, the *Challenger* represented the greatest technological achievement of its age. And like the *Titanic*, it became a casualty of overconfidence. Many experts say that the *Challenger's* final flight should never have been attempted on a morning when freezing temperatures prompted a number of engineers to warn against it.

The potential for disaster is always greatest when humans are striving to explore new frontiers. Such disasters remind us that even when we are most confident of success, failure can happen. Yet the tragedies of the *Titanic* and *Challenger* would have been even greater if they had discouraged people from pursuing their dreams.

Instead, the kinds of dreams that launched the *Titanic* and the *Challenger* have also led to the development of submarines, jet airplanes, rockets, satellites, and other technological achievements. The *Titanic* and *Challenger* can teach us to pursue our own dreams with care. We should advance with confidence, but also with intelligence. Moving forward can be risky. But the risk is decreased when each step is guided by the insights of past failure, and by faith in the promise of the future.

Glossary

aft . . . . At or near the stern, or rear of a ship.

bow . . . . The front part of a ship.

bridge . . . . The high platform on a ship from which the ship is controlled.

bulkhead . . . . One of several walls that divide a ship into water-tight compartments.

commutator . . . . [**COM**-u-tay-ter] An instrument that determines how level a vessel sits in the water.

crow's nest . . . . A lookout platform located high on a ship's mast.

davit . . . . [**DAV**-it] A small crane used for lowering boats or cargo over the side of a ship.

fore . . . . At or near the bow, or front, of a ship.

forecastle . . . . [**FOKE**-s'l] The front portion of a ship's upper deck, in front of the foremast.

founder . . . . To fill up with water and sink.

gangway . . . . The removable passageway from a ship to the dock.

growler . . . . A small iceberg that barely shows above the water.

helm . . . . The wheel or tiller used to steer a ship. Located in the wheelhouse.

hull . . . . The frame or body of a ship.

immigrating . . . . Moving to a new country to live.

Industrial Revolution The rapid, major change in society marked by the use of power-driven machinery. It began in England in the late eighteenth century and dramatically changed the way people lived.

knot . . . . [**NOT**] A nautical mile, approximately equivalent to 1.15 miles (1.85 kilometers).

Marconi . . . . [mar-**KO**-nee] A powerful, sophisticated wireless telegraph that made communication over long distances possible. It was invented by Italian Guglielmo Marconi in 1895.

mast . . . . A tall pole on the deck of a ship. It is used for supporting sails.

Morse lamp . . . . A lamp used on ships for signaling in Morse code.

port . . . . The left side of a ship.

porthole . . . . A small, rounded window in the side of a ship.

quartermaster . . . . A lower-ranking officer who attends to a ship's signals.

robotic . . . . [ro-**BOT**-ik] Robot-like, or like a machine that performs some of the complex acts of a human being.

rudder . . . . [**RUD**-der] A flat, movable plank attached to a boat and extending into the water. It is used for steering.

sonar . . . . [**SO**-nar] The use of sound waves to detect submerged objects.

sound . . . . To measure the depth of water by lowering a weight fastened to a line.

starboard . . . . [**STAR**-berd] The right side of a ship.

steerage . . . . [**STEER**-edge] The areas in the lower decks near the bow and stern of a ship where lowest-paying passengers stay.

stern . . . . The back end of a ship.

sternwheel . . . . The steering wheel of a ship.

submersible . . . . [sub-**MERS**-i-bul] A vessel that operates under water.

teak . . . . A hard wood resistant to weathering, often used for ship furnishings.

tiller . . . . A lever used to steer a boat.

titanium . . . . [ti-**TAY**-nee-um] A light, strong metal, often combined with other metals.

trial . . . . The act of testing a ship to determine how it performs in the water.

wheelhouse . . . . The room on the bridge of a ship from which the ship is navigated.

wireless . . . . The two-way transmission of telegraph signals, using radio waves.

Further Reading

THE *TITANIC*

Ballard, Robert D. *The Discovery of the Titanic.* New York: Warner Books, 1987.

Ballard, Robert D. *Exploring the Titanic.* New York: Scholastic, 1988.

Ballard, Robert D. "How We Found Titanic." *National Geographic*, Vol. 168, No. 6, December 1985, pp. 696-719.

Ballard, Robert D. "A Long Last Look at Titanic." *National Geographic*, Vol. 170, No. 6, December 1986, pp. 698-727.

Ballard, Robert D. "Epilogue for Titanic." *National Geographic*, Vol. 172, No. 4, October 1987, pp. 454-463.

Donnelly, Judy. *The Titanic, Lost—And Found.* New York: Random House, 1987.

Lord, Walter. *A Night to Remember.* New York: Holt, Rinehart, and Winston, 1955.

Sloan, Frank. *Titanic.* New York: Franklin Watts, 1987.

SHIPS AND SHIPWRECKS

Alexander, Anne. *Boats and Ships from A to Z.* New York: Franklin Watts, 1988.

Barrett, N.S. *Ships.* New York: Franklin Watts, 1984.

Brown, Walter. *Sea Disasters.* Reading, Massachusetts: Addison-Wesley, 1981.

Buehr, Walter. *The Birth of a Liner.* Boston: Little, Brown, and Company, 1961.

Lampton, Christopher. *Undersea Archaeology.* New York: Franklin Watts, 1988.

INDUSTRIAL REVOLUTION
AND EARLY TWENTIETH CENTURY

Cowles, Virginia Spencer. *1913: An End and a Beginning.* New York: Harper and Row, 1967.

Eisenstadt, Alfred. *Witness to Our Time.* New York: Viking Press, 1966.

Grant, Neil. *The Industrial Revolution.* New York: Franklin Watts, 1973.

Lane, Peter. *The Industrial Revolution: The Birth of the Modern Age.* New York: Barnes and Noble, 1978.

Other Works Consulted

Chamberlain, E.R. *The Nineteenth Century: Everyday Life.* London: Macdonald and Company Ltd., 1983.

The Concise Columbia Encyclopedia. New York: Avon Books, 1983.

Davie, Michael. *Titanic: The Death and Life of a Legend.* New York: Knopf, 1986.

Gildea, Robert. *Borders and Barricades, Europe 1800-1914.* New York: Oxford University Press, 1987.

Lord, Walter. *The Night Lives On: New Thoughts, Theories, and Revelations About the Titanic.* New York: Morrow, 1986.

Marcus, Geoffrey J. *The Maiden Voyage.* New York: Viking Press, 1987.

McNeill, William H. *A World History.* New York: Oxford University Press, 1979.

Russell, Thomas H. *The Story of the Wreck of the Titanic, the Ocean's Greatest Disaster.* L.H. Walter, 1912.

Wade, Craig Wyn. *The Titanic, End of a Dream.* New York: Rawson, Wade Publishers Inc., 1979.

Index

The Author, Tom Stacey, is a graduate of Michigan State University. He has worked as a reporter and editor for several West Coast newspapers, and now lives and works as a freelance writer in La Jolla, California.

Illustrations by Maurie Manning and Michael Spackman capture the drama of the events described in this book.

Manning majored in illustration at Massachusetts College of Art in Boston and has been a professional children's illustrator for more than six years. Her work appears regularly in such magazines as *Children's Digest, Humpty Dumpty,* and *Highlights for Children.*

A designer and professional illustrator for more than nineteen years, Spackman has experience as both a portraitist and commercial illustrator. He received his training at the High Museum Academy of Art in Atlanta.

Photography Credits
All photos courtesy of the Titanic Historical Society,
P.O. Box 51053, Indian Orchard, Massachusetts 01151-0053